Presented to

. . . .

From

. . . .

Date

. . . .

Books by Kevin Johnson

Early Teen Devotionals

Can I Be a Christian Without Being Weird?

Could Someone Wake Me Up Before I Drool on the Desk?

Does Anybody Know What Planet My Parents Are From?

So Who Says I Have to Act My Age?

Was That a Balloon or Did Your Head Just Pop?

Who Should I Listen To?

Why Can't My Life Be a Summer Vacation?

Why Is God Looking for Friends?

Books for Youth

Catch the Wave!

Find Your Fit[1]

Find Your Fit Discovery Workbook[1]

Look Who's Toast Now!

What Do Ya Know?

What's With the Dudes at the Door?[2]

What's With the Mutant in the Microscope?[2]

To find out more about Kevin Johnson's books
visit his Web site: www.thewave.org

[1]with Jane Kise [2]with James White

00C

WHAT Do Ya KNOW?

NOW THAT YOU'RE A GRADUATE

KEVIN JOHNSON

BETHANY HOUSE PUBLISHERS
MINNEAPOLIS, MINNESOTA 55438

Cover design by Lookout Design Group, Inc.

Published by Bethany House Publishers
A Ministry of Bethany Fellowship International
11400 Hampshire Avenue South
Minneapolis, Minnesota 55438
www.bethanyhouse.com

Printed in the United States of America by
Bethany Press International, Minneapolis, Minnesota 55438

Library of Congress Cataloging-in-Publication Data

Johnson, Kevin Walter

CIP data applied for

ISBN 0–7642–2336–4

To grads everywhere who have
the guts to give their
whole life to God.
Congrats!

KEVIN JOHNSON is the bestselling author of more than a dozen books for youth, including *Can I Be a Christian Without Being Weird?* and *Catch the Wave*. A full-time author and speaker, he served as senior editor for adult nonfiction at Bethany House Publishers and pastored a group of more than four hundred sixth through ninth graders at Elmbrook Church in metro Milwaukee. While his training includes an M.Div. from Fuller Theological Seminary and a B.A. in English and Print Journalism from the University of Wisconsin–River Falls, his current interests include cycling, guitar, and shortwave radio. Kevin and his wife, Lyn, live in Minnesota with their three children—Nate, Karin, and Elise.

For more information about Kevin's books or speaking availability, visit his Web site at www.thewave.org.

Contents

WHO ARE YOU?

PART ONE

YOUR IDENTITY, PURPOSE, AND VISION

So maybe you thought your yearbook photo was ghastly. You might not have graduated with the greatest GPA on the planet. And you might have tripped on the platform as you picked up your diploma. Deep down you might think you're full of flaws: things you've done wrong. Or skills you don't have. Or a dark secret you hardly admit to yourself.

You might try to hide your faults from yourself, your friends, and your family.

You can't hide anything from God. He sees everything.

And He still likes you.

He proved it. A few people might give their life to save a good person, or a friend. No one would think of dying for the flawed, sinful person each of us is—but God did. He proved His love for us by sending Christ to die for us not when we were perfect, but at "just the right time," when we were at our worst.

But God demonstrates his own love for us in this: While we were still sinners, Christ died for us.

—ROMANS 5:8

When you graduate you don't get a pair of superhero long undies to wear while dashing from good deed to good deed. But God's goal for your new existence is this: He wants you to contribute something to this world. After all, "We are God's masterpiece. He has created us anew in Christ Jesus, so that we can do the good things he planned for us long ago" (Ephesians 2:10 NLT).

Your gifts, though, can tempt you to the dark side.

You're probably not planning to do anything dumb or diabolical with your life. But here's the real danger: There's an overwhelming chance that you'll scramble around in selfishness.

If you know what you like and what you're good at, God wants you to set goals and chase them hard—with one caution: You'll only be truly happy if you look beyond yourself. You're way out of bounds if you maneuver through your world only serving your personal happiness.

The happiest grads in America are *not* the ones who keep hitting the snooze button of life. Happy people are ones who find something good they enjoy doing so much that they're willing to work at it. They have a purpose in life.

Whatever you do, do it wholeheartedly as though you were working for your real master and not merely for humans.

—COLOSSIANS 3:23 GWT

God wants you to push, to dare, to try bold new stuff. And He promises that you'll never face a situation overwhelmingly big: "You can trust God, who will not permit you to be tempted more than you can stand. But when you are tempted, he will also give you a way to escape so that you will be able to stand it" (1 Corinthians 10:13 NCV).

Temptation isn't just about urges to have sex, do drugs, or chant satanic rock and roll in your sleep. Your new life is more subtle than that. That wise word also fits temptations to despair, to be selfish, to throw pity parties, and to give up. The verse right before warns to never imagine you can rely solely on yourself. The verse right after cautions against depending on anything other than God.

The writer of Hebrews says the same thing: You can face anything if you face it with God. When you know God is always with you, you're willing to try hard stuff.

God has said,
"I will never leave you; I will never forget you."
So we can be sure when we say,
"I will not be afraid, because the Lord is my helper."

—HEBREWS 13:5 NCV

Truth #1: Big satisfaction comes from doing what God made you to do.

Truth #2: In the adult world that means finding a job that fits you.

No, you don't have to carve in stone right now what you're going to be for the rest of your life. But why is the job thing so crucial? Because in just a few years, you will enter The Working Zone. Of the 168 hours in your week, you will spend

- **60 hours at work, including commute time (more in New York)**
- **54 hours sleeping (six on weeknights, twelve on the weekend)**
- **21 hours eating (more if you wash dishes)**
- **10 hours cleaning (washing clothes, cars, etc.)**
- **10 hours running errands (calling Mom, etc.)**

That leaves about 13 hours a week to do what you want to do, unless . . . *your work is something you want to do!*

Finding work that's actually fun can happen—and the fun doesn't depend on the size of the paycheck. People who like what they do say they find it *interesting*, find meaning in its *bigger purpose*, or find they *do it well*. Really happy people find all three are true. They make a living. Find fulfillment. Better their world.

Adult fun means working hard to find work that aligns with the way God made you.

"For I know the plans I have for you," declares the Lord, "plans to prosper you and not to harm you, plans to give you hope and a future."

—JEREMIAH 29:11

Your parents might edge you into a routine meant to make you an Olympic swimmer, but you dream of being an artist. You want to transplant brains, but your family tells you you're brainless. Your dad expects you to be his clone, but you'd sooner haul garbage. They laugh, they scold, and you get the message: conform or face the consequences.

Conformity can be good. Without parental pressure you would have ditched school, made armpit noises in church, and whined like a baby when you didn't get your way.

Your first out-of-the-house wish might be to find out what you can get away with. But quiz yourself first: *Why* do you want to break the mold? *Who* do you want to please?

Your goal isn't to unnerve your parents or to pursue brat-hood but to run to what God wants. So listen to your parents faithfully. But obey God completely—and chase hard what He designed you to be. Your parents gave you birth, but God made you. You're His.

You saw me before I was born. Every day of my life was recorded in your book. Every moment was laid out before a single day had passed.

—PSALM 139:16 NLT

Jesus taught a surprising principle: If you try to pump life full of things that serve yourself, life deflates. Give yourself away to God and to others, and your life bursts with good things. If you always "look out for number one," unquestioningly "do what feels good," and endlessly "follow your bliss," you'll wind up dissatisfied. Do life how God intends, though, and you'll turn your world into a better place. You'll demonstrate God's greatness to the world. And along the way you'll find what makes you truly happy.

The prime question you want to answer each morning isn't, "How do I want to arrange my life to make myself comfortable?" but, "How do I offer my best back to God and people?"

How? God's answer is *passion*. Passion is caring about something bigger than yourself, important to you and important in the grand scheme of things. It's helping people. Losing yourself in God's higher purposes. Choosing not just to make a living but to make a difference.

Blessed are the people who have these blessings!
Blessed are the people whose God is the Lord!

—PSALM 144:15 GWT

The Old Testament prophet Jeremiah was anything but ordinary when God got through with him. God transformed him from a scared shepherd to one gutsy guy. What made Jeremiah useful to God wasn't his abilities or lack of them, but his obedience to God's plan. Piles of people are talented and smart. Few are like Jeremiah: obedient and available to God.

God chooses and uses ordinary people so that everyone will realize that skills and abilities and talents are gifts from God (1 Corinthians 1:26–31). Whether or not you stand out in a crowd isn't what makes you matter. It's having an obedient heart that lets God lead you in the unique plan He's crafted for you.

"Before I formed you in the womb I knew you, before you were born I set you apart; I appointed you as a prophet to the nations." "Ah, Sovereign Lord," I said, "I do not know how to speak; I am only a child." But the Lord said to me, "Do not say, 'I am only a child.'"

—JEREMIAH 1:5–7

Samson was the strongest guy in the world. But his conceit about his strength was the only thing bigger than his muscles (see Judges 13–16). So when he let his Philistine girlfriend sweet-talk him into revealing the secret of his might, God allowed his enemies to grab him, gouge out his eyes, and toss him in prison to grind wheat like a mule.

Samson became powerful again only when he was tamed—when he remembered that because his strength came *from* God it should be used *for* God. Instead of using his strength for himself alone, he handed the Philistines—a nation at war with Israel—a rather crushing defeat.

When you're smart or skilled you can smear brains in people's faces—or gently clue them in on what you know. When you're strong you can break their thumbs—or use your strength to help them. And when you're funny you choose between pounding people down—and cheering people up.

The strongest people are the ones who don't have to prove their strength.

Then Samson called to the Lord, "Almighty Lord, please remember me! God, give me strength just one more time!"

—JUDGES 16:28 GWT

You know that the Bible makes loads of do's and don'ts plenty clear. These clear commands set obvious boundaries of right and wrong—like "don't lie," "don't kill," "don't steal." Or, as Jesus said, "love God totally" and, "love others as much as you love yourself."

But while God gives huge amounts of direction, you also have huge amounts of freedom. No Bible verse lists your name and tells you that your life will be best spent by becoming a geologist and teaching third grade Sunday school. No Scripture tells you if, where, or when to attend college or what job to take when you finish.

The best way to steer within God's boundaries is *to clue in to what God wants you to do by looking at how you're made*. Look at the rest of God's creation: Eagles soar. Dolphins leap. Cougars blaze. They're doing what they were meant to do. They're at home. They don't try to swap places. You're way more flexible than that, yet God made you with a unique combination of gifts to fulfill a unique role in the universe.

So what are you doing to discover your gifts?

Your first job in life is to learn and stay inside the clear boundaries God put forth in the Bible. Your second job is to learn to function as *you*.

God has given gifts to each of you from his great variety of spiritual gifts. Manage them well so that God's generosity can flow through you.

—1 PETER 4:10 NLT

LOCATING TRUE LOVE

PART TWO

PURITY, SEX, AND DATING

You thought some of your graduation gifts were swell. God's gift of true love is even better.

In marriage a man and woman promise in front of God and His people to love each other for the rest of their lives. To couples who commit themselves to that unending, total friendship with each other, God gives an incredible wedding present: the gift of sexual love.

To honor marriage means to save sex and the things that lead up to it for God's time and place. Your body and emotions get impatient, though. So if you're going to follow God's best for your life—if you're going to wait for sexual love until marriage—you can't be dumb about what you take into your life right now. Movies, videos, music, pornography, daydreaming, dating without boundaries, casual kisses that aren't so casual—all these things add to the pressure you feel.

Some of those things are sips. Some are gallon gulps of poison. All add up. Watch what you drink—what you look at, listen to, and think about.

Marriage should be honored by everyone, and husband and wife should keep their marriage pure. God will judge as guilty those who take part in sexual sins.

—HEBREWS 13:4 NCV

Love is easy to appreciate, hard to understand. It's

like a restaurant that everyone agrees has great food, but where everyone picks a different favorite dish. Guys and girls are attracted to each other in baffling ways, like an eagle floating through the sky, a legless snake slithering across a rock, or a ship navigating the sea.

You never totally figure it out. But it's time to try. You'll drown if you don't know that God has definite plans for how He wants you to get along with the opposite sex.

God isn't bashful. The Bible is blunt. And the parts of the Bible that talk about how men and women should get along weren't scribbled in by monks stuck at the monastery without a date. They were composed by the One who made your body and soul for love.

"There are three things that are too hard for me, really four I don't understand: the way an eagle flies in the sky, the way a snake slides over a rock, the way a ship sails on the sea, and the way a man and a woman fall in love."

—PROVERBS 30:18–19 NCV

Picture this: So-called scientists in white coats brief you before the experiment. "We're testing a new brand of stay-fresh sandwich bags," they inform you. "We've constructed a bag big enough for you to crawl into. We'll zip you inside, place you in a cage with a person-eating tiger, and watch what happens. Rest assured, nothing will happen. You'll be perfectly safe. Our new bag is totally airtight, so the tiger won't catch a whiff of you. And tigers won't eat what tigers can't smell."

"Any questions?" they ask.

Just one.

Are you that stupid?

You wouldn't trust your life to a sandwich bag. Yet your TV tells you to trust your life to a condom. Ads, friends, media—even some doctors, teachers, pastors, and parents—advise you to accept less than God's best.

They're like the people the apostle Paul warned against. They don't want what's best for *you*. They want to drag you into their disobedience, into following evil appetites instead of God.

I urge you, brothers, to watch out for those who cause divisions and put obstacles in your way that are contrary to the teaching you have learned. Keep away from them. For such people are not serving our Lord Christ, but their own appetites. By smooth talk and flattery they deceive the minds of naive people.

—ROMANS 16:17–18

Okay. So you've decided you want to flee people figuring on feeding you to a tiger. But sometimes you don't even know you're being bagged. No one ever bluntly told you how to tell good from evil. So here goes:

Remember God's best: God made sex to be shared by a husband and wife, in order to be physically and emotionally united (Genesis 2:22–24).

Run away from the rest: Sex isn't for people not married to each other. Sex isn't a party sport. Sex isn't a dare, a drunken game, or a contest to get as much as you can. Sexual contact is never for people of the same sex. The sex God invented isn't selfish, hurtful, violent, forced, or controlling. Sex isn't something adults or teens do to children. Sex isn't a spectator sport for the screen or a magazine. And even when "two consenting adults" say they "love each other," sex and all the groovin' things that lead up to it are out-of-bounds before marriage.

God's kind of sex is never dirty. It's private, but never something you have to keep secret or be embarrassed to talk about with your most wise, godly, trusted counselors.

Don't be stupid. Don't let anyone toss you to a tiger.

But run away from the evil young people like to do.
Try hard to live right and to have faith, love, and peace,
together with those who trust in the Lord
from pure hearts.

—2 TIMOTHY 2:22 NCV

Let's get practical. Gals: When Paul wrote that women should dress modestly, he wasn't picking on you. He knew that people—*especially* guys—are tempted by what they see. When you choose swimwear spun from a single spool of dental floss you might as well mail the guys invitations to your birthday suit. To dress every day in "appropriate clothes that are modest and respectable" you don't have to wear a bag. But you don't want to brag. Whenever you bait boys with your outward appearance you're asking them to see less than the real you.

Guys: That's *no* excuse for you to grab with your eyes or your hands what isn't yours. When you start to want what you can't have, stare somewhere else (Matthew 5:27–30). Turn off the TV. Toss the magazine. Hang up the phone. Run away. Beg your girlfriend to cover up or find yourself a new girlfriend. Shut down the software.

Back to both of you: When you buy a present for a friend, you don't wrap it up and then kick it down the street or hurl it around a crowd. You would never hand a friend a torn and dirty gift. And a half-unwrapped present spoils the surprise.

You're the gift. Your spouse is the recipient. Take care of the present.

I want women to show their beauty by dressing in appropriate clothes that are modest and respectable.

Their beauty will be shown by what they do, not by their hair styles or the gold jewelry, pearls, or expensive clothes they wear. This is what is proper for women who claim to have reverence for God.

—1 TIMOTHY 2:9–10 GWT

Anything that is good, praiseworthy, true, honorable, right, pure, beautiful, and respected—that is what should fill your mind. Read those words again. How much of what you read—and listen to and think about—during a day passes those tests? What are you doing to slam the lid shut on things that don't, and to open yourself up to things that do?

No sane person spends the day playing in a garbage Dumpster. You might, though, play in mind garbage, pulled in by the need for friends, an escape, or excitement.

Trust those needs to God in prayer. He will meet your needs in a healthy way, and give you a peace that will help you dive out of the Dumpster.

Don't worry about anything; instead, pray about everything. Tell God what you need, and thank him for all he has done. . . . Fix your thoughts on what is true and honorable and right. Think about things that are pure and lovely and admirable. Think about things that are excellent and worthy of praise.

—PHILIPPIANS 4:6, 8 NLT

You'd know you were in the wrong place at the wrong time with the wrong crowd if cops busted down the doors of the house you were in and shot in tear gas.

But people and places and situations don't have to be so unmistakably evil to be just as risky. The Bible, for example, makes clear that Christians shouldn't be "unequally yoked," roped together with non-Christians. Attachments like going together, dating, marriage—probably even being best friends—with people who are cold toward God sooner or later will keep you from obeying God (2 Corinthians 6:14).

But that doesn't mean you should run and hide from non-Christians. When the Pharisees criticized Jesus for spending time with sinners—including the lowest life-form of that society, tax collectors—Jesus retorted that He was like an army medic rushing to help the wounded and dying. He went where He was needed most.

Jesus wasn't making an excuse to have the out-of-bounds fun He would miss if He stuck close to "nice" people. His goal was to invite people to meet God. What's yours?

Jesus answered them, "Healthy people don't need a doctor—sick people do. I have come to call sinners to turn from their sins, not to spend my time with those who think they are already good enough."

—LUKE 5:31–32 NLT

You don't live in a bubble. Your world, you might have noticed, isn't very Christian. Your Christian friends aren't always around. You aren't even fitted with a pressurized space suit to keep you from exploding when you venture out alone into spiritual nothingness.

Like every other Christian, you'll face temptations to do wrong. (That's why the Bible calls temptation "common to man.") But maybe the biggest temptation you'll face is this: to stop paying attention to God. To do well without Him. To ease Him out of your life. To be like the fool who says, "There is no God" (Psalm 14:1). That fool doesn't mean that God doesn't exist. He means that God doesn't matter.

Often it's you, God, and a temptation—no one looking, no Christian friends to pull you back. In those moments, the decision to obey God—to make Him matter—is yours alone.

God always provides a way to choose Him. You may not see it at first. But choosing to hunt for His way out is your first step in choosing to make Him matter.

No temptation has seized you except what is common to man. And God is faithful; he will not let you be tempted beyond what you can bear. But when you are tempted, he will also provide a way out so that you can stand up under it.

—1 CORINTHIANS 10:13

When you blow it as a Christian, you can't take back hurt you've caused. You still live with the consequences of messing up. Sin still offends God. But God makes a way to repair your relationship with Him and start over *right now*. A verse in 1 John tells how: "If we confess our sins, he is faithful and just and will forgive us our sins and purify us from all unrighteousness" (1:9).

That's part of what Paul meant in another spot in the Bible about "forgetting the past and looking forward to what lies ahead." If you admit your sin to God, He forgives you and picks you up so you can press on toward the goal of knowing Christ completely.

Don't ever give up on following Christ just because you fall down. There's no such thing as a Christian who never stumbles. Real Christians are the ones who get up and go on.

No, dear friends, I am still not all I should be, but I am focusing all my energies on this one thing: Forgetting the past and looking forward to what lies ahead, I strain to reach the end of the race and receive the prize for which God, through Christ Jesus, is calling us up to heaven.

—PHILIPPIANS 3:13–14 NLT

Way back in ancient times the people of Israel had mind-boggling experiences of God. He saved them from slavery in Egypt and led them to freedom with a cloud and pillar of fire. He gave them Moses' leadership and fed them with bread from heaven. Even so, they turned away from what they knew. They chased evil instead of good, worshiping idols (Exodus 32:1–6), sinning sexually (Numbers 25:1–9), and grumbling against God (Numbers 21:4–6).

You don't have to try sin to know that it's wrong and that sooner or later it hurts. The Bible, your parents, and other Christians tell you evil isn't the fun it's cracked up to be. Don't blow them off.

Experience is a great teacher—especially someone else's rotten experience. You're smart to learn from your own mistakes. But you're brilliant to learn from others' blunders. It's their pain, your gain.

These things happened to them as examples
and were written down as warnings for us.

—1 CORINTHIANS 10:11

FACTS IS FACTS

PART THREE

TRUTH, FAITH, AND WISDOM

God doesn't expect you to swallow truth whole. He wants you to chew.

Back in the Bible when Philip told Nathanael that Jesus was God's Son come to save the world, Nathanael was skeptical. But Nathanael also accepted Philip's invitation to come and see Jesus. That's different from refusing to believe something no matter what the evidence.

Jesus told Nathanael that He had seen him under the fig tree—a customary spot for studying Scripture. That supernatural knowledge was a sure wow, but more than that, it meant that Nathanael knew where to look for answers. He was like the Bereans (Acts 17:11), who heard the message Paul preached about Christ "with great eagerness and examined the Scriptures every day to see if what Paul said was true."

Nathanael wasn't crabby. He wasn't making excuses. He loved truth enough to ask questions, chew on the answers, and find life (2 Thessalonians 2:10).

As they approached, Jesus said,
"Here comes an honest man—a true son of Israel."

—JOHN 1:47 NLT

You can find truth in lots of places. God lets you learn from parents whose heads aren't empty and from grandparents and other older people whose lives have been full. He allows you to study history so you don't repeat people's mistakes, and to learn about science and the arts so you won't be stupid about your world.

But the Bible's truth is unique. It's inspired by God—"God-breathed"—so its truth is completely flawless. The Bible is a measurement for everything else that claims to be true—a friend's words, a musician's lyrics, an author's ideas, a screenwriter's view of life. It corrects you when you're wrong and encourages you when you're right. God designed the Bible for you to read and apply with other believers so you can discover Him and understand yourself and your world.

Scripture is God's perfect, reliable written word. It's the first and last test of who to listen to.

All Scripture is inspired by God and is useful to teach us what is true and to make us realize what is wrong in our lives. It straightens us out and teaches us to do what is right.

—2 TIMOTHY 3:16 NLT

Even if you *trust* the Bible, you can still *misunderstand* it. You can use the Bible because of its reliability. But you'll only get what the Bible means if you're careful how you interpret it. You're bound to become nuts if you read more than is there, read less than is there, or focus on itty-bitty issues and miss the big ones.

Here's the truth: Some parts of the Bible aren't quite as ready-to-read as a road map. The details aren't always as straightforward to figure out as you'd like.

Yet three quick reading rules can help you keep the main points straight.

Rule One: Read to Obey. Jesus tells us to grab hold of His truth and test it. He promises that those who try it out will confirm its truthfulness.

Rule Two: Read What It Actually Says. Don't add to it. Don't take away from it. Remember to study hard.

Rule Three: Read for the Big Stuff. Easy test: Any spirituality or theory of God that misses or misshapes or minimizes Jesus is automatically wrong.

To the Jews who had believed him, Jesus said, "If you hold to my teaching, you are really my disciples. Then you will know the truth, and the truth will set you free."

—JOHN 8:31–32

Trying to find truth in some places is like trying to find lost change in a toilet. It may be there, but it's not worth the dig.

Disgusting? You bet. But so is swishing through the swirl of waste you find in loads of TV shows, videos, tunes, concerts, magazines, books, comics, and computer games—not just the violence, nasty language, and "adult situations," but the arrogance, sarcasm, and selfishness.

That isn't smart stuff. If you're looking for wisdom—for truth, reality—which leads to life, there's a better place to look. Music or a movie may voice what you feel or express a truth about life. But it doesn't teach the knowledge of ultimate truth and reality that satisfies through and through. Only God's wisdom does.

Wisdom is treasure worth searching for. It's worth crying out for. And God is *the* place to get it. Don't bother looking for platinum in a Porta Potti.

Cry out for wisdom, and beg for understanding. Search for it like silver, and hunt for it like hidden treasure. Then you will understand respect for the Lord, and you will find that you know God.

—PROVERBS 2:3–5 NCV

You're goofed up if you get up in the morning, study yourself in the bathroom mirror, and then go away without fixing your face and brushing away your morning breath.

There's only one thing that's more goofy: reading the Bible and then walking away and ignoring what it says. God wants you to develop your ability to hear and do something about His words. When you obey what you hear, it's like you've turboblasted your ears clean. "Do not merely listen to the word, and so deceive yourselves. Do what it says" (James 1:22).

When God guides you through the Bible, He speaks through His *commands*—His clear-cut, no-way-around-them decrees of right and wrong. He also guides you through *conviction*, making you sure of what's best as you offer yourself to Him (Romans 12:2).

"If you love me,
you will obey what I command."
—JOHN 14:15

It's easy to believe God when things go well. You're sure of it: *God is good. God is powerful. God is right. God loves me. God tells the truth.*

It's not so easy to believe when life explodes. That's when you wonder why people at work treat you rotten, why your family fights, why school busts your brain. When you can't figure out why God doesn't fix it all, you're tempted to start thinking differently about Him: *God's evil. He's weak. He's mistaken. He doesn't care. He's trying to trick me.*

When circumstances grew tough for Jesus and He was tempted to stop believing and stop obeying His Father, He fought back with Scripture. Jesus countered Satan's statements point by point with verses from the Old Testament (from Deuteronomy 8:3, 6:16, and 6:13). Jesus applied Scripture to His life, and Satan fled.

You can't shoot laser missiles at your thoughts, or at your enemies. But God's words are your weapon. You build up your ammunition every time you study your Bible. And you fire when you say, "Hey, brain. Don't listen to that lie. It's not true. God says . . ."

That's the only way you'll win.

The devil said to Jesus, "I will give you all these kingdoms and all their power and glory. . . . If you worship me, then it will all be yours." Jesus answered, "It is written in the Scriptures: 'You must worship the Lord your God and serve only him.'"

—LUKE 4:6–8 NCV

People nowadays want to string you up by your First-Amendment-protected vocal cords if you suggest that they are in any way *wrong*. Posters on one campus put it this way: "It isn't wrong to think you're right. But it's wrong to think others are wrong." Especially when it comes to religion, if you dare claim you know ultimate, total truth, you might as well wear a sign saying, "KICK ME. I'M INTOLERANT." You're labeled arrogant, offensive, and unloving.

Big problem.

Christians are to be all-loving. That's different, however, from all-inclusive, all-accepting, and all-tolerant. Anyone who has read even a few paragraphs of the Bible knows that God purports to have revealed through His Word what's true and what's not.

He says that He alone is God—which means no one else gets to wear "God" on his name tag. *He says that we can know Him through Christ alone*—which means no other lord will do. *He tells us how we should follow Him*—which means He alone is smart enough to make the rules for life.

You will have some false teachers in your group.
They will secretly teach things that are wrong—
teachings that will cause people to be lost.
They will even refuse to accept the Master,
Jesus, who bought their freedom.

—2 PETER 2:1 NCV

Disagree. But disagree gently.

Right now society is afraid to deal with disagreement. It's downright hostile to anyone who claims he's right and others are wrong. But the truth is, it's intellectually, morally, and spiritually cowardly to ignore big issues and hope for everyone to "just get along." In one way, we *can't* get along with people who lead us into lies.

Don't pick fights. Don't go rude and crude. Instead, arm yourself with truth—God's truth—and fight on the battlefield of ideas. And do it "with gentleness and respect." You can't tell folks about how Christ is Lord in your life with your fist. Or with harsh words. Or with anger in your face.

But in your hearts set apart Christ as Lord.
Always be prepared to give an answer to everyone who asks you to give the reason for the hope that you have. But do this with gentleness and respect.

—1 PETER 3:15

Even when you bust loose and tell people about Christ, they don't always listen. To everything you say they throw up objection after objection. Most people you'll meet, though, who say they disagree with the truths of Christianity don't know the Bible they're arguing with. Let the Bible speak for itself:

- Believing in God is for wimps (2 Corinthians 11:23–27—Read Paul's diary. He wasn't exactly a wuss).

- Christianity is fine for you. But there are a lot of other good religions. Jesus was just another teacher (John 14:6—Jesus himself claimed to be the only way).

- God is fine. I hate church. It's a bore and I don't need it (Hebrews 10:23–25—We need each other to get strong).

- Why should I listen to you? Christians are hypocrites—they always say one thing and do another (Isaiah 29:13–14—God gets disgusted with hypocrites more than we ever will).

- God loves everyone. He wouldn't send anyone to hell (Psalm 14:1–3; Romans 3:23, 6:23—God will judge each of us whether we think He will or not).

- Science proves the Bible isn't true or the Bible is full of myths. Why should I believe it? (2 Timothy 3:16—Ask them to name specific myths or points where science contradicts the Bible. Often they can't offer any)

- God doesn't exist. I've never gotten an answer when I've prayed (Psalm 14:1; James 4:3—God's reality isn't limited to our knowledge of Him).

For the word of God is living and active. Sharper than any double-edged sword, it penetrates even to dividing soul and spirit, joints and marrow; it judges the thoughts and attitudes of the heart.

—HEBREWS 4:12

WHO GOD IS AND WHAT GOD'S DONE

PART FOUR

LOVE,

GRACE,

AND

SALVATION

Some enemies of God are easy to spot, as though they carry bazookas. Their wrongdoing—their sin—is obvious: They fight, kill, lie, or steal. They misuse sex. They disobey authority and beat up people. Or they hurt their own bodies by drinking or abusing drugs.

The sins of other people are harder to see. Even nice people with polite outsides, the Bible says, can have rotting insides. They may have a bad attitude toward God—by refusing to bow before His greatness or to applaud His absolute goodness. People make their own plans for life and mistrust God's wisdom. By that standard, God says that *all* human beings have messed up and sinned—including you. We're all rebels (Romans 3:23).

God can't stand evil. And He's the King. So look at it this way: As rebels we've been booted out of the palace. But God doesn't hate us. He wants us close to Him. And it's our own fault if we stay out in the cold, because God has created a way—through Jesus—to welcome us back in.

Drop your weapons and come inside for the party.

You are not a God who takes pleasure in wickedness.
Evil will never be your guest.

—PSALM 5:4 GWT

God thinks that compared to you, even gold is worthless. When God wanted to reestablish a friendship with you, the price that God paid was the death of His Son, Jesus. Cash registers can't *ka-ching* that high! Yet that's the price tag God puts on you and everyone else on earth. That's how much He thinks you're worth. That means no one should ever be tagged as a reject, and you should never feel that way about yourself.

Everyone is equally valuable to God. No one is on sale. No one is an ugly shirt with six markdowns on his price tag that says, "You're worthless. No one wants you." Your price tag says the same thing as all the others in the world: "Jesus loves me and died for me."

You were bought, not with something that ruins like gold or silver, but with the precious blood of Christ, who was like a pure and perfect lamb.

—1 PETER 1:19 NCV

We don't always want the truth. We believe lies—and tell them—to keep life pleasant.

Unlike us, God swears to be honest in everything He says. He doesn't tease. When He tells His people that they can seek Him and know Him, He means it. And He says that He—and no one else—knows perfectly what is right.

Big promises. But we can be sure they're not big lies. We would be stupid to trust what God says if He were out busting knuckles or breaking hearts. He's not. His honest words are backed by honest actions.

God's ultimate promise is to be God for everyone who trusts Him: "There is no God apart from me, a righteous God and a Savior."

And when God sent Jesus, He gave us the ultimate proof that He means what He says.

For this is what the Lord says—he who created the heavens, he is God; he who fashioned and made the earth, he founded it; he did not create it to be empty, but formed it to be inhabited—he says: "I am the Lord, and there is no other."

—ISAIAH 45:18

You're caught between a rock—and *the* Rock (Isaiah 26:4). You face humiliation and rejection if you ignore the demands of your friends. Yet you know God will be less than thrilled watching you do wrong and abuse yourself, others, and Him.

You feel squashed either way. So what's the use of picking sides?

Jesus bluntly told His disciples—His followers—that for Him to obey God's plan would mean He would be mocked and killed on the cross. He was still determined to obey God.

And Jesus said that in the same way anyone who wants to follow Him must "deny himself" and "take up his cross." To follow Jesus is to swap your way for His way—completely. It's to obey Him even when it hurts—even when you feel like you've been pierced with nails and all you can do is twist in pain. Daring to stick with Jesus sometimes feels like you've been hung up to die. That's tough stuff. But here's why to choose Jesus' side: Jesus makes an unbreakable promise that His way leads to life.

Then he called his disciples and the crowds to come over and listen. "If any of you wants to be my follower," he told them, "you must put aside your selfish ambition, shoulder your cross, and follow me. If you try to keep your life for yourself, you will lose it. But if you give up your life for my sake and for the sake of the Good News, you will find true life."

—MARK 8:34 NLT

You believe in God, right? He loves you, and you're supposed to love Him back. That means walking away from every sin. No sweat, right? Give yourself to God with all your might, mind, and strength. No problem, right? Yep, you meet folks every day able to pull that off, don't you?

Hardly. Being human means messing up. Sooner or later you love yourself or things around you more than you love God. Every time you put yourself or your desires above God, that's sinning. If you loved Him supremely in all things, you wouldn't do that. If you need to rid yourself of every ungodly habit AND love God perfectly *before* He smiles at you, you're in deep trouble. So is every other human being.

That's why what the Bible calls "grace" is *unmerited*

favor. Because of Christ's death, God accepts you the way you are. He wants to grow you, but He starts with you where you're at. Grace is complete. God's approval is total. It can't be bought, purchased, earned, or merited. You can't suck up to God. You can't impress Him. You can't buy His love. If you've got to give something to get it, it isn't *grace*.

The Spirit and the bride say, "Come." Let each one who hears them say, "Come." Let the thirsty ones come—anyone who wants to. Let them come and drink the water of life without charge.

—REVELATION 22:17 NLT

A radical change happens between you and God when the wall of sin and separation crumbles. Picture the universe as a high school and God as Principal Over All. Now stretch your imagination beyond what you ever probably saw in school: You can go to God's office—His presence—without fear. Jesus took your punishment on the cross and won you total friendship with God.

Before becoming a Christian, we rebel, hate rules, make excuses for sin, and fear death and hell—the ultimate expulsion. After accepting Jesus as Savior and Lord, we learn friendship, trust, forgiveness, and openness to correction. We look forward to eternity in heaven with God, our best friend.

Don't be afraid to go to God. His door is always open.

We can enter through a new and living way that Jesus opened for us. . . . So let us come near to God with a sincere heart and a sure faith, because we have been made free from a guilty conscience.

—HEBREWS 10:20, 22 NCV

You don't have to be a sleaze queen or an ax murderer to have offended God. When you grasp that God is good and sin is evil and how totally repulsive *all* evil is to God—well, you can start to feel like rat chow.

Here's the good news: We walked away from God, but while we were still stuck in sin He took the first step toward us. He didn't make people get perfect before He would be their friend.

The religious leaders watching Jesus hated His friendliness toward sinners. They mocked His choice of a crooked tax collector to be His follower and despised His dinners with sinners. But those who sneered at Jesus for chumming with the bad guys were blind to their *own* badness.

They didn't think they needed a spiritual doctor, so they pushed Jesus away. They stayed sick. It was the ones who admitted they needed a spiritual doctor who let Jesus near and got well.

But God demonstrates his own love for us in this:
While we were still sinners, Christ died for us.

—ROMANS 5:8

The Bible is clear that God's wrath comes because of a *choice*. God has made himself obvious through the world He has made, so we have no excuse for not acknowledging Him. In fact, hell gives us eternity for what we've chosen in this life: a long walk away from God (Romans 1:18–31). Like Billy Graham has said, "God will never send anybody to hell. If man goes to hell, he goes by his own free choice. Hell was created for the devil and his angels, not for man. God never meant that man should go there." Dante, author of the *Divine Comedy*, wrote, "If you insist on having your own way, you will get it. Hell is the enjoyment of your own way forever."

Hell is a choice because God offers us a way out—a way out of judgment, a way out of the banishment from His presence that makes hell *hell*.

How do you choose that way out?

Admit that you've rebelled. "For all have sinned and fall short of the glory of God" (Romans 3:23). Tell God you've sinned.

Accept God's terms of surrender. "For the wages of sin is death, but the gift of God is eternal life in Christ Jesus our Lord" (Romans 6:23). Tell God you know that Christ died in your place—He died even though *you* are the one who deserves death.

Ask God for His new life. "I tell you the truth, whoever hears my word and believes him who sent me has eternal life and will not be condemned; he has crossed over from death to life" (John 5:24). Tell God thanks for forgiving you and for filling you with power to live a life on *His* side of the cosmic battle.

Your new life can begin now. It's your choice. And being close to Him lasts forever.

I give them eternal life, and they shall never perish; no one can snatch them out of my hand.

—JOHN 10:28

THE REAL AND THE FAKE

PART FIVE

GOD'S WAY VS. THE HUMAN WAY

You don't always have to choose between pleasing people and pleasing God. Your friends may be great for you, supporting God's best choices and echoing God's voice. But it's a delusion to think that you never have to rebel against your friends to follow God.

Look at it this way: Peers deserve your friendship; they don't deserve to run your life.

God will be around long after people around you laugh at you, turn their backs on you, and walk away. And—this is hard—pleasing God is infinitely more important than satisfying any human being. Jesus talked about peer fear when He said, "Do not be afraid of those who kill the body and after that can do no more. . . . Fear him who, after the killing of the body, has power to throw you into hell" (Luke 12:4–5).

Blunt. But true.

Do you think I am trying to make people accept me? No, God is the One I am trying to please. Am I trying to please people? If I still wanted to please people, I would not be a servant of Christ.

—GALATIANS 1:10 NCV

Jesus blows aside our ideas of the value of power and prestige. Even two thousand years ago He refused to play to the crowd just to score first in the polls. He came on His own terms.

The facts are these: Jesus gave up the splendor of heaven and was born as a helpless baby (Luke 2:12; Philippians 2:6–7). He made friends with outcasts and sinners (Matthew 9:10–14). He hung out with children (Luke 18:16). He went to out-of-the-way, dangerous places (John 4). He cried (John 11:35). He refused to wield power to serve himself (Matthew 26:53). He came as a servant (Matthew 20:28). He forgave His enemies (Luke 23:34). He sweat blood in grief (Luke 22:44). He died an agonizing death on a cross (John 19:17–18).

But *why*? What good did it do for Jesus to act like that?

Jesus' goal was to show us God. Not a god manufactured by media spin, but THE REAL GOD.

Jesus didn't just look *like* God. He *is* God. So when Jesus came to earth, He showed once and for all what God is like. Jesus "became a human and lived among us. We saw his glory—the glory that belongs to the only Son of the Father—and he was full of grace and truth" (John 1:14 NCV).

"It's the same way with the Son of Man. He didn't come so that others could serve him. He came to serve and to give his life as a ransom for many people."

—MARK 10:45 GWT

Lemmings are tough little ratlike rodents that live in northern Europe. When their colonies get too crowded, millions of lemmings leave their homes in spectacular mass migrations. Sometimes they run into the sea. None of them bother to find the answer to the one question that really matters: Is this a good idea?

No. Lemmings can't swim.

They don't intend to drown themselves. They're just looking for a nicer, less crowded place to live. Lemmings are stupid. Lerts, on the other hand, ask smart questions.

If someone tries to lead a lert along a line of living that looks like it lacks logic, a lert likes to learn more: Who's leading this migration? Where are we going? Is it a good place to live?

Lerts have learned to discern lies. Unlike lemmings.

Don't be a lemming. Be alert.

I am sending you out like sheep among wolves. Therefore be as shrewd as snakes and as innocent as doves.

—MATTHEW 10:16

God is no build-your-own-tostada bar. You can't pick the guacamole but flick the onions, or choose the cheese but lose the beans, making God fit your taste. While you're free to build a tostada to *ooh* and *aah* over, it's not okay to make God into what you think is best.

God wants you to know Him exactly as He is, as He's shown himself to be.

God also determines the what, when, where, and how of following Him. When it came to worship, for example, He told His people what to get rid of, where and how to build a temple, what to eat, and how to sacrifice animals—in so much detail that it makes you want to tell God to calm down. Yet the rules helped God's people stand out from their neighbors and to understand that God wants pure, obedient, disciplined followers.

And God made a big point. He's the one who determines what's important and what's not, what's right and what's wrong, what's real faith and what's fake. He's in charge. He's God.

Never worship the Lord your God in the way they worship their gods. The Lord your God will choose a place out of all your tribes to live and put his name. Go there and worship him.

—DEUTERONOMY 12:4–5 GWT

Jealousy doesn't end when you get what someone else has, because you'll always find someone else who still has more. Even the beautiful and bulked-up people feel left out. Miss Americas claw and whine to get their own talk shows, and Super Bowl winners turn into armchair-quarterbacking couch potatoes. And they hate people who have what they want, whether it's more looks, muscles, money, or popularity.

The only hope is to be happy with what *you* have. God won't do plastic surgery on your looks or your life to make you into someone else. He does a heart transplant to redo your attitude.

The apostle Paul told his friend Titus that before we know God, we're wrapped up in malice (a desire to harm or spite others) and envy (unhappiness at what someone else has or can do). Yet when we accept God's kindness we begin to see we have everything we need most—God's acceptance, His forgiveness (we're "justified by His grace"), the promise of living in eternal paradise with God, and friendship right now with His Holy Spirit.

Compared to that, what others *do have* that you *don't have* is nothing.

But when the kindness and love of God our Savior was shown, he saved us because of his mercy. It was not because of good deeds we did to be right with him. He saved us through the washing that made us new people through the Holy Spirit.

—TITUS 3:4–5 NCV

The right-here-right-now success of bad people is never the whole story. In God's judgment at the end of time, evildoers will be punished, but those who follow God will romp like frisky calves set free from their pen. You can be one of those calves—

rompy, rompy, rompy—havin' a stompin' good time. Jesus himself (the "sun of righteousness") will heal you so you forget you were ever hurt or discouraged.

So it isn't that God doesn't notice right-here-right-now wrongs, or that He doesn't feel your pain. Just the opposite—that's why He sent Christ to end evil, to give people a chance to turn to Him. God is patient, though, and holds off His scorching punishment.

When you feel overcome by evil, be patient. Remind yourself that God sees you and won't forget your faithfulness.

"But for you who revere my name, the sun of righteousness will rise with healing in its wings. And you will go out and leap like calves released from the stall. Then you will trample down the wicked . . ." says the Lord Almighty.

—MALACHI 4:2–3

Mumble something nasty to yourself about an enemy and it's a bad attitude. Say it to someone else and it's gossip. Shout it at your enemy and it's picking a fight. Tell it to God and suddenly it's prayer.

How can you get away with that?

Because it's *prayer*. It's pouring out all the thoughts and feelings of your heart to God. It's asking *God* to do His thing. It isn't dishing out justice with your own hands—like an egghead paying back cruelty inflicted on him, or a madman stalking and murdering a doctor who does abortions. And it isn't begging God to carry out your whims. It's pleading to Him to halt evil and give evildoers the punishment they deserve.

Old Testament believers were a bit foggy about life after death, so their prayers against enemies usually scream, "Crush them NOW, God. Don't miss your chance!" Yet the New Testament is clear that some of the payback for evil—God's judgment, or His "vengeance"—often won't happen until the end of time (Revelation 19:11–21).

And that's okay. God gives even awful people a chance to respond to His kindness. His concern for now is more to reach them than to roast them (2 Peter 3:7–9).

Are you still impatient for God to toast your enemies this afternoon? Not so fast. Think about it. Should He be so quick to punish you?

Lord, battle with those who battle with me.
Fight against those who fight against me.

—PSALM 35:1 NCV

Someday you might possess the success of a Bill Gates. You might perch at the tip of the tallest office tower in the world. But there still will be Someone above you.

Whether your kingdom consists of a bunk bed, half a bedroom, and a few video games—or a dorm room, a microwave, and an '84 Honda—or cars, condos, corporations, techno-toys beyond imagination, and the largest CD collection in the world—you're not master of the universe. You don't even rule your own life.

There's no escape: You serve *somebody*. The Bible says you're a slave either to what's wrong or to what's right (Romans 6:19), either to death or to life (Romans 8:6), either to Satan or to God (Ephesians 2:1–10).

Trying to run your own life is like leaping off an office tower. You won't fly. Life without God is a death-spiral as sure as gravity. But to "hate" life and give yourself back to God—that means to stick close to Him, obeying His commands—sends you soaring.

Growing up into a post-graduation life isn't getting free to finally rule the roost. It's your chance to choose for yourself to follow Jesus—to fly with the real Master of the Universe.

All those who want to be my disciples must come and follow me, because my servants must be where I am. And if they follow me, the Father will honor them.

—JOHN 12:26 NLT

You aren't on the playground anymore. And your mommy isn't around to rescue you from neighborhood bullies. So how are you going to solve your people problems?

Sometimes you can stand up for your rights by speaking truth (Ephesians 4:15), relying on the authorities God put in place to make things right (Romans 13:1–5), or running for help when you can't fix a problem yourself (Matthew 18:15–17).

But other times there's no escape. You'll get the stuffing beat out of you. You'll get stomped on. You'll get steamrollered.

Meekness ain't weakness. Meekness is gentle, self-controlled strength. Meekness means being something better than the bullies who beat up the world. God is on the side of the gentle, and Jesus tells us who *won't* win the ultimate popularity and power contest—the proud, strong, aggressive, harsh, and tyrannical who suck life from others.

Inheriting the earth means God gives a prize—someday, some way—for every pint of blood you give up. So it's clear who the real losers are.

Blessed are the meek, for they will inherit the earth.

—MATTHEW 5:5

Jesus didn't insist you had to be poor. He *did* say there are lots of things more important than having tons of possessions (Matthew 6:19–34). He didn't say God will accept you more quickly if you give away your camel. After all, you become God's friend not because of what *you do* but because of what *Jesus did*. Obeying lets you *experience* God's care, not buy it.

Yet Jesus pointed out that what you possess can possess you. He chatted once with a rich young man who had done everything right—except love God above anything else. The man hadn't strangled anyone, stolen anything, or spewed at his mother. But when Jesus invited him to follow—yet to ditch his luggage first—he couldn't bear to leave his horde of wealth behind.

Lots of things in life are good. But they aren't good if they go extreme and keep you from following Jesus—like trying too hard to be popular (Galatians 1:10), overestimating the size of your brain (1 Corinthians 1:28–29), doing what's right merely to show off for others (Matthew 6:2–4), or getting too busy for God (Luke 10:40–42).

To follow Jesus, you have to let go of what's good when it keeps you from grabbing what's best.

Jesus answered, "If you want to be perfect, go, sell your possessions and give to the poor, and you will have treasure in heaven. Then come, follow me." When the young man heard this, he went away sad, because he had great wealth.

—MATTHEW 19:21–22

WE GOTTA GIVE IT ALL

PART SIX

DISCIPLESHIP,
ATTITUDE,
AND
CHRISTLIKENESS

When you submit to God, you give Him your will. You say, "God, I want what *you* want." You declare that you're done drifting. You reject sin and get rid of what the Bible calls "doublemindedness," halfhearted living. When you begin to understand the deadly dangers of sin you "grieve," "mourn," and "wail" for what you've done wrong. Powerful feelings.

Moving out on your own is one of the wildest rivers you'll ever run. God wants you to decide *now* to follow Him completely. You can write yourself a reminder of what you decide in the margin of this page. Date it. Sign it. Celebrate it. And stick with it.

But the result of giving your all to God is clear: God will lift you free and set you paddling straight. If you don't decide, then you've chosen to drift. And maybe drown.

So give yourselves completely to God.

—JAMES 4:7 NCV

If you were put in a room with six live people and six dead people, you wouldn't have a hard time telling which were which. Sure, from across the room you might mistakenly think someone was snoozing, and there are tragic cases where only God knows whether a person still lives inside the shell of a comatose body. But you can usually distinguish dead bodies from live ones.

Christians are spiritually alive. They're the ones who are moving. Growing. Non-Christians are spiritually dead.

Now, you only see their outsides. You can't peer into their guts for positive proof their faith is or isn't even a little bit alive. Only God can. But their lack of vital signs makes you suspicious. Here's what the Bible says a real Christian looks like:

- **Real Christians are reconciled—they've become friends with God (Romans 5:1).**
- **Real Christians are rescued—they're owned by God (Colossians 1:13–14).**
- **Real Christians are under reconstruction—they're being changed from the inside out by God (Titus 2:11–12, 14).**
- **Real Christians are responsive—they're listening for God's commands and carrying them out (1 John 2:3, 5b–6).**
- **Real Christians are resilient—they get up and go on after they mess up (1 John 1:8–9).**

You can detect them by the way they act, just as you can identify a tree by its fruit. You don't pick grapes from thornbushes, or figs from thistles. A healthy tree produces good fruit, and an unhealthy tree produces bad fruit.

—MATTHEW 7:16–17 NLT

If anyone had a claim to a lavish welcome as God's messenger, it was Jesus himself. He was God in human flesh. He deserved earsplitting praise, rich accommodations, one-of-a kind recognition.

That wasn't the path He chose. He told his followers, in fact, that He "did not come to be served, but to serve, and to give his life as a ransom for many" (Matthew 20:28). If we were Jesus we'd expect to soak in a hot-tubbed limo. He came expecting a carry-and-wear device of death: the cross.

When you remember Who's in charge of this planet, you go into your world as a servant. Listen to what Paul wrote: "Your attitude should be the same as that of Christ Jesus: Who, being in very nature God, did not consider equality with God something to be grasped, but made himself nothing, taking the very nature of a servant . . . he humbled himself and became obedient to death—even death on a cross!" (Philippians 2:5–8).

Only Jesus could die on the cross. But you have the opportunity in all you do to be a servant—to sacrifice for the sake of others.

But he was wounded for the wrong we did;
he was crushed for the evil we did. The punishment, which made us well, was given to him, and we are healed because of his wounds.

—ISAIAH 53:5 NCV

If you let people turn you into a too-spiritual-for-real-life doormat, then you won't be able to give when it really matters.

Christ gave because He was strong, not because He was weak.

No one walked all over Him. No one stole anything from Him. He *chose* to give, in both life and death: He "made himself nothing." He "humbled himself." Here's a strange one: Even when He was about to be taken by force to be beaten and crucified, He made it clear to His killers that He was dying by choice.

Being robbed and giving a gift have the same result: You pay a price. But when you give by choice, people don't see a fool. They see Christ.

Surely you know I could ask my Father, and he would give me more than twelve armies of angels.

—MATTHEW 26:53 NCV

Living totally for God doesn't mean you spend every spare moment being sucked dry by the needs of others. You get to enjoy God's creation, fun times with friends, learning for the heck of it, the ups and downs of families. In other words, you get a balanced life.

And Jesus modeled that life for you. When He was tired, He rested. When the crowds overwhelmed Him, He left. When He received bad news, He retreated with His best friends. If Jesus had time for weddings, boat rides, visits with close friends, and His relationship with God, then so do you.

And you have to be filled up to serve. Ditch the image of servants of God who wear themselves out, neglect their families, and die of exhaustion. Jesus said He came not just so you'd have life, but abundant life—a life with plenty of resources and incredible richness (John 10:10). Not *riches*, but *richness*. You can't concentrate on the needs of others if you're forever trashed. You don't want to feel like someone else is driving your car in the race of life—and you're just along as a passenger, ready to lean out the window and heave when the curves come.

So how do you create a balanced life? Accept the fact that you're a complicated person. God expects you to take care of yourself.

Then, because so many people were coming and going that they did not even have a chance to eat, he said to them, "Come with me by yourselves to a quiet place and get some rest."

—MARK 6:31

Don't be shocked when life gets hard. Just because something takes effort doesn't mean you're stupid or lazy or uncoordinated or unspiritual. It means God is working on you.

God uses your struggles to discipline you—to *train* you—to make you strong, tough, and more like Him. That's not necessarily because you've been bad, but because He knows you can be better.

You practice to get good at anything. You need to practice to master life, and to become a strong Christian.

God doesn't put you into training because He's a cruel coach who laughs while you run laps. He knows what it takes to make you mature—when to go easy and when to push hard—and His discipline is always perfectly planned for your good.

God's discipline hurts. But it works.

We don't enjoy being disciplined. It always seems to cause more pain than joy. But later on, those who learn from that discipline have peace that comes from doing what is right.

—HEBREWS 12:11 GWT

Up until now, your parents have set your rules. You may not have noticed it, but the protection of your parents has probably sheltered you from the cold facts of life: If you're sassy, you get fired. If you're a jerk, you get bounced out of your apartment. If you're lazy, you starve.

When you leave home you don't escape rules. Instead of parents, you get professors and roommates and bosses—and then a spouse and kids to answer to. In fact, there's no such thing as "running your own life." When you get to be out on your own, you actually get only two choices: *I will follow and obey God* or *I will choose another god.* Trying to run your own life means leaving what you think is a prison and checking into a zoo. It might look like a nice place to visit, but you wouldn't want to be locked up there. Happiness and freedom aren't found in busting loose but in choosing to enjoy God and His will for you (Psalm 37:3–4). It's better to enjoy your place as a daughter or son in God's family than to be a baboon at the zoo.

"Choose for yourselves this day whom you will serve. . . . But as for me and my household, we will serve the Lord."

—JOSHUA 24:15

The sight of a beautiful animal dead on the side of a road is sick. Just as sad is seeing someone flattened by carelessly spoken words.

Roadkills happen when a driver moves so fast that he slams into an animal before he can stop. When you speak without thinking, you hit someone before you reach the brakes. Your words kill.

Make your words helpful, not harmful. Joking about people isn't helpful. Neither are sexual jokes—they don't help your mind or show others respect. If you need to say something negative, it should be to build up, not rip down. That means talking directly to the person, not behind his or her back (Matthew 18:15).

Just because an animal walks across the road doesn't mean you can hit it. Just because something is true doesn't mean you should say it. Slow down and let someone live.

Don't use foul or abusive language. Let everything you say be good and helpful, so that your words will be an encouragement to those who hear them.

—EPHESIANS 4:29 NLT

Jesus was totally God. But He didn't act like His Royal Too-High-to-Help-Out-ness. Born a baby and trained as a carpenter, He grew up and did good wherever He went—healing, feeding, making miracles, feeling people's joys and pains. And in the end, Jesus went to the cross. Even when He died for *us*—a bunch of witless people who'd wasted earth—He never grumbled that His unbeatable abilities were being splattered into nothingness like a kicked-over paint bucket.

When you think you're too good to hang with or help certain people—with anyone, anywhere—you're claiming a superiority God's Son scorned. Jesus didn't deny His greatness. He didn't gulp back His goodness. Instead, He used that great goodness to help people.

You don't have to bash yourself or neglect your own needs. But you can choose to count others better than yourself. To look out for more than your own interests. To serve people who need your help more than you need it yourself.

Just like Jesus.

When you do things, do not let selfishness or pride be your guide. Instead, be humble and give more honor to others than to yourselves.

—PHILIPPIANS 2:3 NCV

THE ULTIMATE FRIEND

PART SEVEN

PRAYER,
TRUST,
AND
GOD'S WILL

With so many voices screaming at you about what you should do with your life—tonight, tomorrow, and for the next twenty years—which ones do you believe? How do you know who is wrong—or who is right? Who speaks truth? Who spouts lies?

Who should you listen to?

The easy way is to give up and follow whichever voice is the loudest. That isn't the only way. Jesus invites you to follow Him, wanting you to answer to His voice. He helps you sort out the other voices. He shows you truth from lies, good from bad, real from fake.

God's voice isn't the loudest, because He respects you too much to scream at you. But listen up. You'll discover that He's the One worth listening to.

He calls his own sheep by name and leads them out. When he has brought out all his own, he goes on ahead of them, and his sheep follow him because they know his voice. But they will never follow a stranger; in fact, they will run away from him because they do not recognize a stranger's voice."

—JOHN 10:3–5

You're in pain. You would settle for less than a miracle. You just want a little something to take the edge off your agony. And you wonder why God doesn't respond to your generous offer to become a missionary to Ukarumpa in exchange for a little help now.

But nothing happens. You think God has said, "Forget it, slimeball. Chew dirt!" and you get aggravated. *Hello, God! Can't you see I'm hurting? Quit ignoring me. Why won't you answer me?*

He has.

God doesn't sleep or go to lunch. And He doesn't put a price on His services. He doesn't hear you because of *your* promises to Him but because of *His* promise to you: You belong to Him. He sees your problems and hears your prayers. But He answers prayers the way He knows is best (1 John 5:14–15).

He doesn't always say, "Yes." Yet He's not necessarily saying, "No." Sometimes He says, "Wait" or, "I'll answer, but not the way you think." When you trust God, He renews your strength—to walk, to run, to fly.

But the people who trust the Lord will become strong again. They will rise up as an eagle in the sky; they will run and not need rest; they will walk and not become tired.

—ISAIAH 40:31 NCV

In the Bible a guy named Asaph expected that God would fix his dire loneliness instantly. He no doubt thought that as a follower of God, he was a friend worth having. He should be liked, popular—and included. In time, God surely gave him friends, but for a while God let him be alone.

Asaph found that God sometimes lets you feel lonely to remind you that all you really have is God, and that He is all you need. You might be alone in a dorm room—or surrounded by a crowd in a cafeteria, gagging on food you're too sad to eat. Who will you depend on? Friends move, or you just change. Who will you hang out with?

In the middle of being lonely, Asaph came to a simple conclusion: *God* is always near. When you have no one else, you have God, and He's enough.

Yet I am always with you; you hold me by my right hand. You guide me with your counsel. . . .
Whom have I in heaven but you?
And earth has nothing I desire besides you.

—PSALM 73:23–25

You aren't a pain to God when you ask Him to meet your needs. In fact, Jesus encourages you to ask, expecting an answer. "Whoever asks, receives."

Jesus uses a bizarre comparison to show God's eagerness to answer your prayers. No father, He says, would serve his child a snake instead of a fish, or a scorpion instead of an egg. Jesus' point is that if an earthly father, who sins and makes mistakes, can muster that much compassion, then you can be confident, knowing that your perfect heavenly Father will be unfailing in giving you good gifts.

"So I say to you: Ask and it will be given to you; seek and you will find; knock and the door will be opened to you."

—LUKE 11:9

Prayer is like breathing. You'd better do it all the time, but at times you need to stop and think about it. Prayer is an attitude that lasts all day, but there are times when you want to settle down long enough to just pray.

Whatever you're trying to do with your life, prayer is where you start. God gives you some major reasons to pray:

Pray and tell God you want what He wants. If God is the one you've put in charge of your life—and if He's the one who powers all you do—it's a good idea to tell Him you're ready to get to work.

Pray and tell God how great He is. You can't ignore God's goodness. You don't have to keep quiet about it.

Pray and invite God to break through and change the world. You can ask that the people you talk with will be willing to listen. For Christians to get along so that the world recognizes Christ in us. And for a bigger view of God.

Pray continually.

—1 THESSALONIANS 5:17

Jesus did say, "Ask whatever you wish, and it will be given you." But here's the crucial part: *If* you remain in Him and His words remain in you, *then* God will give what you ask. "To remain" means to be like a vine that stays connected to the branch. If you "remain," you draw life from God, resulting in obedience to God. To have Christ's words in you means you're shaped by His promises, values, and priorities.

That doesn't mean God answers only the prayers of ultraspiritual people, or that any one of us could ever earn His favor. It just means that if you live close to God, you'll want what God wants for you, and He'll gladly grant that request. You'll want things that make you more like Christ so you show God's greatness.

Sometimes you won't realize you're asking for something God doesn't want for you. And once in a while it won't make any sense to you why God didn't answer a prayer the way you thought He should. Yet only God can see the best possible answer to your every request.

If you remain in me and my words remain in you,
ask whatever you wish, and it will be given you.

—JOHN 15:7

Nothing is scarier than facing a roomful of people who think you're a dork. Even if you want to be friends, something about you makes them hate you. They might not like what you do. They might not like *you*.

You could talk like them, act like them, mangle people like them, have ungodly sex or inhale like them—all to keep from looking stupid and feeling alone. You could give up and give in. You could suck up and let people control you. Or you can stick with the Friend who sticks with you and let Him make you strong.

God promises that the same power that raised Christ from the dead lives inside you if you belong to Him (Romans 8:11). His Holy Spirit remakes you to want and to be able to do what's right (Philippians 2:13). That's a "spirit of power" and a "spirit of self-discipline." But He also promises to make you able to face others with a "spirit of love" (2 Timothy 1:7). It's what makes you fearless and forgiving even when others hate you.

Following God doesn't make you timid. It makes you tough.

Each time God said, "My gracious favor is all you need.
My power works best in your weakness."
So now I am glad to boast about my weaknesses,
so that the power of Christ may work through me.

—2 CORINTHIANS 12:9 NLT

Of all the rulemakers in your world, only God possesses all three of these things: earth-shaking power, flawless wisdom, and total love. The result? Perfect judgment about what's right and what's wrong, what builds up and what rips down. Not one of His rules is dumb or dated, and not a single one is meant for anything less than your good.

That's what God's "faithfulness" is all about. People's nastiness won't destroy you if you grasp the perfection of God's ways—His "laws," "precepts," "statutes," and "commands." Threats, sarcasm, and laughter loom over you only until you see their idiocy compared to God's boundless wise care.

If your law had not been my delight, I would have perished in my affliction. I will never forget your precepts, for by them you have preserved my life.

—PSALM 119:92–93

Nobody with more than half a brain ever bought the Doors' classic lyric "Hello, I love you, won't you tell me your name?" Love is based on knowledge.

It's a problem to say you love God yet not dig to know all you can about Him.

You probably know a lot about *what God does*: He made you. Died for you. Lives in you. You likewise are probably learning *what God is like*: Loving. Just. Faithful. You may have thought less about *who God is*. God's actions and character don't come from nowhere. Maybe no one has ever taught you *what He's about* at the core of his being: Eternal. All-powerful. All-knowing. Morally flawless. Unchanging. Triune.

Christians' most basic conviction about God is that He's *one of a kind*. There's only one God, and He's not taking applications for a replacement. God *is* God.

Always *has been* God. Always *will be* God. Period.

"I am the Alpha and the Omega—the beginning and the end," says the Lord God. "I am the one who is, who always was, and who is still to come, the Almighty One."

—REVELATION 1:8 NLT

WHAT'S YOUR PRIORITY?

PART EIGHT

PEERS AND POPULARITY

Wanting everyone on campus to like you ruins you. It forces you to fit the expectations of the ones you want to impress—to be someone you're not, to do things you don't want to do, and to say things you normally wouldn't say. Besides that, your popularity lasts only as long as your beauty, brains, or brand of comedy are tops. Then you're out and someone else is in. It's better to find one good friend who "sticks closer than a brother" than a crowd of fans who control and use you.

You might not meet those close friends at parties. Back in the Bible Jonathan and David met as young men after David walloped the giant Goliath and was brought before Jonathan's father, King Saul. They met because David did what was right (1 Samuel 18:1–4). Ruth and Naomi were stuck together by tough times (Ruth 1). The apostle Paul became Timothy's friend and mentor when Timothy began ministry as a teen (2 Timothy 1:6).

Some people may never accept and appreciate you the way you are. But you can ask God to help you find one real friend in the midst of the mass.

A man of many companions may come to ruin, but there is a friend who sticks closer than a brother.

—PROVERBS 18:24

The Bible shows two kinds of wise men and women: James says that real wise guys are "pure;

then peace-loving, considerate, submissive, full of mercy and good fruit, impartial and sincere." They live a "good life" full of "deeds done in the humility that comes from wisdom."

The scoop on fake wise guys is scary. James says that when people are full of "bitter envy and selfish ambition," life is full of "disorder and every evil practice." And a little bit of fake wisdom gets hugely nasty: it's "earthly, unspiritual, of the devil" (James 3:13–17).

The point? Friends that seem not so bad can be really not good at all.

You can be a bottom-feeder, getting bloated and having lots of cruddy friends. Or you can look for the best friends. But you are what you eat.

Whoever walks with the wise will become wise;
whoever walks with fools will suffer harm.

—PROVERBS 13:20 NLT

Not all peer pressure is beer pressure—a big push to swill alcohol, torch your brain on drugs, misuse sex, or disrespect authority.

Everybody needs good peer pressure—a healthy dread of what other people think. Good peer pressure is the deodorant of life. It stops life's little stinks.

Still, there's an even better peer pressure. The best peer pressure helps you choose God and His good ways. You ditch evil best—and chase God the hardest—

when you hang with peers who want to follow God. You need their best pressure to push and pull you to God's greatest stuff.

As iron sharpens iron, a friend sharpens a friend.

—PROVERBS 27:17 NLT

You may be all grown-up, but you still don't like getting laughed at. Or ignored. Or being uninvited to parties. So maybe you choose to duck between your conscience and the people around you. Maybe you aim to be good enough to calm your conscience but not so good you get noticed.

That's settling for playing in the shadows when you could be living in the light. It's living a lie when you belong to the truth. Peter points out how your belonging to God affects how you live: "Dear friends, I urge you, as aliens and strangers in the world, to abstain from sinful desires, which war against your soul. Live such good lives among the pagans that, though they accuse you of doing wrong, they may see your good deeds and glorify God on the day he visits us" (1 Peter 2:11–12).

You don't always fit with your world because your real home is heaven—why would a living soul feel at home in a graveyard? When you follow what's right—God's way—the good life you live gets noticed. And God gets the glory.

You are chosen people, a royal priesthood, a holy nation, people who belong to God. You were chosen to tell about the excellent qualities of God, who called you out of darkness into his marvelous light. Once you were not God's people, but now you are. Once you were not shown mercy, but now you have been shown mercy.

—1 PETER 2:9–10 GWT

Wolves manage to knock off animals a lot larger than themselves by separating individuals out from the herd. It's survival of the fittest. The circle of life. Food chain facts.

Here's how that ugly reality relates to wacky spiritual belief systems: A Christian who has been separated from the herd of God's people is easy prey for cults. Maybe he wandered off because he got hurt—who hasn't been smashed by God's people? Or she left because church was boring—who hasn't wheezed through a snoozer sermon? Cults shower that person with concern and compassion, and before long they've got another faithful follower. Happens all the time.

No church is perfect. Nope—you don't want First Church of the Forever Frozen. God is cool—not frozen. Nor do you need Swinging Chandelier Christian Center. Jesus will energize you—but He shouldn't need a spatula to scrape you off the ceiling.

Yet lots of churches will grow you God's way. If we don't hang together, we're like infants "tossed back and forth by the waves, and blown here and there by every wind of teaching and by the cunning and craftiness of men in their deceitful scheming" (Ephesians 4:14).

Get those pictures of a Christian separated from the rest of God's people? Animal hunted down. Baby bobbing on ocean. Not pretty.

Better hang with the herd.

Let the peace of Christ rule in your hearts, since as members of one body you were called to peace. And be thankful.

—COLOSSIANS 3:15

Encouraging each other isn't group hugs. It isn't forcing gooshy feelings the way you wring the last bubble of toothpaste from a tube. Encouragement is inspiring someone's courage. It's helping a friend climb higher.

It's possible for any of us to be duped into thinking sin looks good and God looks bad. The remedy? Daily doses of reality dropped kindly on us by other Christians.

Encouragement means reminding a friend *who God is*: God never makes dumb rules (Psalm 19:7–9), and He's good and loving in everything He does (Psalm 145:17). Encouragement means reminding a friend *what's right*: obeying authority (Colossians 3:20), taming your tongue (James 1:26), speaking with purity about the opposite sex (Ephesians 5:3–4), plus lots of other things you know God wants. And encouragement means reminding a friend that *you'll make it together* (2 Timothy 2:22).

Encourage each other every day while you have the opportunity. If you do this, none of you will be deceived by sin and become stubborn.

—HEBREWS 3:13 GWT

Before you go to battle in the desert you slip into sand-colored clothes and coil a rattlesnake around your head. If you fight in the Arctic you sport snowstorm white and hang icicles from your nose. And for combat in the jungle you wear green and black fatigues complemented by face paint and twigs in your hair. It's simple survival.

If camouflage is good enough for the marines, it's good enough for you. Right?

You'll change a lot more than your clothes if your social survival strategy is doing whatever it takes to fit, belong, blend in with friends old and new at the bar. You pretend to like stuff you hate and to detest stuff you love. You talk behind people's backs—out of both sides of your mouth. You get talked *into* and *out of*. And you devour anyone you think resides lower on the food chain. With winks, nods, and inside jokes you're two-faced. Deceitful. A fraud.

At least two people know the truth. You. And God. When you hide the real you no one can laugh at you. But neither can anyone truly like you.

A good-for-nothing scoundrel is a person who has a dishonest mouth. He devises evil all the time with a twisted mind. He spreads conflict.

—PROVERBS 6:12, 14 GWT

Some people say that every family is a mess. Here's the truth: Some families get along well most of the time. Many get along well at least some of the time.

You may not have come from one of those families. You might have grown up with divorce, violence, or alcohol or drug abuse. Your parents might have worked too much. You might even have been beaten up or sexually abused. If that's you, find a counselor or pastor or teacher to talk to. You're not alone. And you won't make it alone.

Whatever kind of family you come from you can still control how *you* act. It's easy to be nice to friends. But you no doubt let yourself do things to your parents and brothers and sisters you would never do to your friends.

Whether you're still in your family's face every day or far away, it doesn't have to be that way. Paul says that the love and forgiveness God has for you is something you can pass on to the world around you—including your family. You don't have to sass, spew, or slug and turn your family into enemies. As far as it depends on you, you can be a friend (Romans 12:18).

You aren't weird if you get along with the people you grew up with. You're weird if you don't try.

Be kind and loving to each other, and forgive each other just as God forgave you in Christ. You are God's children whom he loves, so try to be like him.

—EPHESIANS 4:32–5:1 NCV

"God called us to live and reach out to others," Donn—a college freshman—says about what he's learned about sharing Christ. "I've learned that people who are most difficult are the ones Christ came for. He didn't come for people who think they're healthy and 'good,' but for the ones that everyone else sees as worthless."

Christians sometimes act like an igloo—toasty on the inside and frosty on the outside. Or a clique—a circle turned inward. Jesus made the same point Donn does. When religious people accused Jesus of being too tight with sinners, He responded that it was the sinners who needed Him (Matthew 9:12–13). Half of your job is to stick together with other Christians. The other half is to spread out. It's the only way you can keep God's News from getting stuck with you.

"So go and make followers of all people in the world. Baptize them in the name of the Father and the Son and the Holy Spirit. Teach them to obey everything that I have taught you, and I will be with you always, even until the end of this age."

—MATTHEW 28:19–20 NCV

ETERNITY MEANS HEAVEN OR HELL

PART NINE

WHICH

DO

YOU

CHOOSE?

Jesus said that at the end of time He will sort between those who know Him and those who don't (Matthew 25:31–46). John wrote that we would all face a judgment before "a great white throne" (Revelation 20:11–15).

Paul's second letter to the Thessalonians makes clearer what all this means, in maybe the plainest warning in the whole Bible: "This will happen when the Lord Jesus is revealed from heaven in blazing fire with his powerful angels. He will punish those who do not know God and do not obey the gospel of our Lord Jesus. They will be punished with everlasting destruction and shut out from the presence of the Lord and from the majesty of his power" (2 Thessalonians 1:7–9).

The *when* of punishment is the end of time, when Christ comes back.

The *what* of punishment is separation from God's awesome and wonderful presence. A lake of burning sulfur is a picture of why hell is *hell*: God isn't there.

The *who* of punishment are those who don't know God—those who haven't received God's offer of forgiveness in Jesus. Accepting that free gift is what it means to "obey the gospel of our Lord Jesus."

For the wages of sin is death, but the gift of God is eternal life in Christ Jesus our Lord.

—ROMANS 6:23

Surrendering to God may seem to you like the right thing to do. Or maybe not.

Even back in Bible times people thought they didn't need to choose God's side anytime soon. They weren't in any hurry to stop being God's foe and accept the friendship and forgiveness offered in Jesus.

Peter wrote that people would scoff at the promise of Christ's return. He assured his readers that judgment and joy were sure to come (2 Peter 3:3–9). He also pointed out this: Christ's "slowness" to show up is an opportunity for human beings to stop fighting against Him. There's one huge reason for God's delay (2 Peter 3:8–9).

God has given time. God might continue to give time—that's His choice. The hitch is that you could feel you have all zzzzz time in zzzzz world.

If you snooze, you lose.

You know very well that the day of the Lord will come like a thief in the night.

—1 THESSALONIANS 5:2

Words give us only the skinniest glimpse of heaven. But they tell us this:

We'll like where we are. Jesus once told His disciples He would soon go away. They bawled. He reassured them that He was leaving to improve their eternal home (John 14:1–3).

We'll like who we are. When Jesus brings heaven home and brings us home to heaven, we will see God as He is and be made like Him (1 John 3:2). Our flawed, decaying earthly bodies will be transformed into heavenly bodies. They'll be different. But somehow the same. Except they'll last forever (1 Corinthians 15:35–49).

We'll like who we're with. That's considerably deeper than holding hands and humming *Kum Ba Yah* (Revelation 21:3–4). For those who believe in Jesus, the penalty of sin has already vanished—we're forgiven. So has the power of sin—we can start to live as new people. In heaven even the presence of sin will be gone. We can be together now and forever. With not a jerk in sight.

We'll like who God is. Like the angels, we will see God's face (Matthew 18:10). Whatever else heaven is, it's a chance to live in God's presence. God wants *you* in heaven with Him. And if God is your friend, there's no better place to be.

> *Nothing impure will ever enter it [heaven, the city of God], nor will anyone who does what is shameful or deceitful, but only those whose names are written in the Lamb's book of life.*
>
> —REVELATION 21:27

Not to burst any bubbles, but when it comes to predicting the swift and immediate end of the world, we've been here before. People—and yes,

Christians—are going around in circles. We're coming back to a spot we've already seen. It's a cosmic case of been there, done that.

Not long ago a book predicted that 65 million Americans would soon starve to death. Famine would spread from coast to coast as the population of the United States outstripped the land's capacity to produce food.

The prediction was made in Paul Ehrlich's *The Population Bomb*. Publication date? 1968. When was America supposed to starve to death? The 1980s.

Reports of the death of the planet were greatly exaggerated. You are living proof Ehrlich was wrong. Here's the point: Just because Christians say the end of the world is coming pronto doesn't mean you should believe them.

Test everything. Hold on to the good.

—1 THESSALONIANS 5:21

During the Great Distress (Tribulation) at the end of time, the Antichrist rampages against anyone who follows God. But a second factor makes the Great Distress so greatly distressing: God punishes everyone who chooses to follow anyone but Him.

A world of sin isn't what God had planned. He won't allow this half-full/half-empty world to go on forever. Evil has refused to go down without a fight. And so humanity's ultimate rebellion brings God's ultimate response.

Why is God so mad? What finally makes Him act? Why the Great Distress?

His wisdom knows it's time to *expose evil*.

His righteousness compels Him to *punish evil*.

His compassion moves Him to *destroy evil*.

At the end of time, people disobey God worse than ever. They disbelieve His love. They distrust the rules His kindness designed. Human rebellion is alive and kicking hard. So God grabs evil like a cowboy grabs a bull by the horns. This bull, though, won't be tossing the cowboy up in the air, flinging him to the ground, or stomping on his chest. This bull is going down. There will come a day when God says, "TIME IS UP! ENOUGH CHANCES! EVIL WILL STOP!"

He made a promise by the power of the One who lives forever and ever. He is the One who made the skies and all that is in them, the earth and all that is in it, and the sea and all that is in it. The angel promised, "There will be no more waiting!"

—REVELATION 10:6 NCV

Jesus is coming back. It's the heart of the Bible's message about the end of the world.

And there won't be any mistaking the arrival of Jesus. When Jesus left earth after His crucifixion and resurrection, He made His exit from the Mount of Olives, outside Jerusalem. As Jesus spoke to His disciples "he was taken up before their very eyes, and a cloud hid him from their sight" (Acts 1:9). The disciples were gawking at the sky when two angels suddenly appeared to them. " 'Men of Galilee,' they said, 'why do you stand here looking into the sky? This same Jesus, who has been taken from you into heaven, will come back in the same way you have seen him go into heaven' " (Acts 1:11).

No one will miss the sky-filling fireworks. Jesus is coming back in the same way He left. On the clouds. With the sky shaking. The sun and moon darkened. Stars falling from the sky.

And no one will miss what Jesus' entrance means. God will boom from His throne, "It is done!" (Revelation 16:17). When Jesus arrives, *it means God's perfect kingdom is here.*

For as lightning that comes from the east is visible even in the west, so will be the coming of the Son of Man.

—MATTHEW 24:27

Don't freak. Don't fret. Christians agree that Jesus is going to come back and swoop us home, even if we do debate—loudly—exactly when that will happen.

You have to put this on a scale of 1 to 10 of "things worth pondering." A biggie question like how we're made right with God is definitely a *10*—better get the answer straight. What color to paint the bathrooms in your church basement is a *1*—despite the fact that churches have split over seafoam green vs. desert taupe. Things like forms of baptism, gifts of the spirit, and free will vs. determinism might be a *6* or *7*—not a matter of whether you're a Christian or not, but biggish in how you run your Christian life.

So how important is the *timing* of Christ's return? In the grand scheme of things, probably about a *3*. Watch out for people who try to make it a *10*.

And there's one fact about Christ's coming you can be indubitably sure of: Knowing where Christians are during the events of the end isn't the great question of life. It's nice to predict we'll already be in heaven. It's probably smart to brace to be on earth.

But more important than where *we* are is where *you* are. Sooner or later Christians will get to heaven. Where will you be?

It's your choice whose side you'll stand on. And which spot you'll spend eternity in. You can be *with* the Toaster of All Things Evil. Or *in* the toaster.

The Lord will come from heaven with a command, with the voice of the archangel, and with the trumpet call of God. First, the dead who believed in Christ will come back to life. Then, together with them, we who are still alive will be taken in the clouds to meet the Lord in the air. In this way we will always be with the Lord.

—1 THESSALONIANS 4:16–17 GWT

It's insane for any human being not to know what the Bible teaches about hell. Hell sounds harsh. But we wouldn't have it any other way.

Hell shows the evilness of evil. Hell isn't just for Olympians of evil. None of us has a hard time qualifying for the hell team. Jesus tells us who is "outside the city" of heaven: occultists, the sexually immoral, murderers, idolaters, and everyone who loves and practices falsehood (Revelation 22:15). "Idolaters" and "falsehood" catch all of us. But in case you're wondering if you're good enough at being bad, Paul's writings lump together "big" sins with all the "little" sins we're so good at—making it clear that without the forgiveness we gain in Christ, none of us is fit for heaven (Galatians 5:19–21). By the hugeness of the punishment we can gauge the hugeness of our crimes.

Hell displays the rightness of God. So long as sin is allowed to go on, we're likely to see it as no big deal. We're likely to see God as a doof, a stupid old fool. And that would be silly on our part. His perfect love and perfect knowledge roll together to give Him perfect judgment (Revelation 16:5–7).

Hell fulfills justice. No sin is hidden from God. At the end of time murderers will no longer go free. Abusers will be found out. All the ghastliness of our hearts will be revealed. Bad guys big and small will fall when God pays back trouble to those who dish it out (2 Thessalonians 1:6).

Hell gives you patience. Evil triumphs ten thousand times a day in your world. Know what? Whatever grief you get for being a Christian—for acting, thinking, and feeling the way God wants you to—will be paid back. God sees. He's on your side. He may take longer to punish evil than you like, but His judgment *will* come (2 Peter 2:9).

Hell confirms our freedom. Now, that's freaky. But it's true.

> *But I will show you whom you should fear: Fear him who, after the killing of the body, has power to throw you into hell. Yes, I tell you, fear him.*
>
> —LUKE 12:5

Revelation is the Bible's scariest stuff. It's probably meant to be. It shows people the do-or-die seriousness of making the right choice: Jesus.

Big points: Worship only God (Revelation 14:11), hang tight to Jesus (14:12), endure persecution patiently (12:17; 13:7), and God will one day zing you home to heaven (7:13–17).

But God doesn't want you worried for the wrong reasons or running scared of the wrong person. He wants to straighten out stuff you've seen in bad movies shown late at night—or in church basements.

Here's truth: No one will take the mark of the beast, for example, by accident. The mark is a sign of a deliberate choice to worship a world leader other than God, to offer your life and allegiance to a religious, economic, and political system other than Jesus (Revelation 16:2).

Clear on that? You don't get the mark by letting the quickmart guy scan the bar code on your Twinkies. Or by using an ATM or a debit card. Or by getting tattooed or silicon-chipped in your sleep. More than that, *no one who truly loves God will be mistaken about what the mark means.* Remember? By this point in future human history, God's Good News about Jesus has been preached to the whole planet. The world is clear on who God is (Matthew 24:14). The Beast openly defies the one true God, and those who take the mark openly ditch that real God and obey the Beast instead.

He said in a loud voice, "Fear God and give him glory, because the hour of his judgment has come. Worship him who made the heavens, the earth, the sea and the springs of water."

—REVELATION 14:7

You won't enjoy a long road trip if you haven't a clue where you're headed. If all you're sure of is that your backside is glued to a car seat you'll feel duped, dragged to who-knows-where. Not having some understanding where you're headed, why, and what you'll see along the way turns the ride into a chore and a bore. And you'll yawn, snooze, and snore if you finally get to your destination and no one explains what you're looking at.

Reading the Bible is like flipping through postcards to show us our destination—actually, to show us what *we* will look like when our journey is done: Our relationship with Christ will change us completely. We'll be pure, blameless, filled with the fruit of righteousness. Our lives will glow with God. People will see what He's done in us and worship Him. And on our trip we'll stick together and learn how to live best.

The trip has already begun. God is in the driver's seat. He promises to get us to the goal. And we don't have to guess where we're going.

I'm convinced that God, who began this good work in you, will carry it through to completion on the day of Christ Jesus.

—PHILIPPIANS 1:6 GWT

EVANGELISM IS GIVING IT AWAY

PART TEN

HOW ELSE THEY GONNA KNOW?

When you "receive Christ," you receive God's free gifts: Forgiveness. Membership in God's family. A life close to your Lord. That's the package the Bible calls "salvation." You're saved from the penalty and the eternal power of sin.

There's more. Jesus didn't stay on the cross. He rose from the grave. He appeared a dozen times to a total of some six hundred people. Forty days after He rose He ascended to heaven, shot into the sky, and returned to His Father. Yet when He disappeared into the clouds He didn't say, "Show's over! Fun while it lasted! Go back to normal! Forget I was here!" Jesus didn't rip into history and then roll the closing credits like Porky Pig: "That's all, folks!"

So here's the point: God's activity on planet Earth didn't stop when Jesus died on the cross. And He wants you to find your place in His plan to change the world!

God has made us what we are. He has created us in Christ Jesus to live lives filled with good works that he has prepared for us to do.

—EPHESIANS 2:10 GWT

God isn't into obnoxious words of faith. You don't have to wear a sign, pin, bracelet, or T-shirt—or stick a fish onto the tail end of your roadster. But you do need to be okay with being known as someone who belongs to God.

You know God. You belong to Someone great. Don't be afraid to say it, even when others think you're crazy.

"Do not worry about how you will defend yourselves or what you will say, for the Holy Spirit will teach you at that time what you should say."

—LUKE 12:11–12

A big hunk of Christians don't like to think bad about anyone. All of us want to be kind. Tolerant. Fair. But being wrong about God carries a high price. Knowing the truth of the true Gospel is heaven-and-hell important.

Paul described people who reject the true God like this: "The god of this age has blinded the minds of unbelievers, so that they cannot see the light of the gospel of the glory of Christ, who is the image of God" (2 Corinthians 4:4). Alternative religions can't see the real Christ. They're blind to God.

That's the need. God has appointed you and other Christians to meet the need: "We do not preach ourselves, but Jesus Christ as Lord, and ourselves as your servants for Jesus' sake. For God, who said, 'Let light shine out of darkness,' made his light shine in our hearts to give us the light of the knowledge of the glory of God in the face of Christ" (2 Corinthians 4:5–6). God put His light in you so you can shine in dark places.

Be a light for other people. Live so that they will see the good things you do and will praise your Father in heaven.

—MATTHEW 5:16 NCV

God powers you up every time you study the Bible or learn from other Christians. The Holy Spirit also makes you achieve things beyond anything you could normally do.

God's Holy Spirit is with the people you talk to before you get to them. He'll be there after you leave. Besides that, He's working inside of you. Depending on God means you're being what He calls you to be—then leaving the fixing to Him.

"But you will receive power when the Holy Spirit comes on you; and you will be my witnesses in Jerusalem, and in all Judea and Samaria, and to the ends of the earth."

—ACTS 1:8

A cult is a group that claims to be Christian—often that they *alone* are the true Christian Church—but denies the core teachings that define the Christian faith.

Read that a few times. While there are many *signs* of a cult, this is what really *defines* such a group. They may teach that God came from another planet (the Mormons), that only 144,000 people will enjoy heaven (Jehovah's Witnesses), or that their leader has the right to slip children deadly cyanide (People's Temple), but this is where the mayhem starts.

They claim to be Christian. Yet when it comes to the doctrines that define faith—beliefs that separate Christianity from all other religions—they dismiss them. They insist on different beliefs.

So what are these whopper doctrines about which cults teach whopper untruths? Watch out when you find groups messed up on three teachings central to Christianity: 1) who God is, 2) what God has done in Jesus, and 3) how we know this (the Bible).

Whoever teaches false doctrine and doesn't agree with the accurate words of our Lord Jesus Christ and godly teachings is a conceited person. He shows that he doesn't understand anything.

—1 TIMOTHY 6:3–4 GWT

Before Jesus was taken up into heaven, He didn't promise to send a postcard every day that said "wish you were here." He didn't post a new email address. Instead, He said He would stick with believers through His Spirit *living in you*. The Holy Spirit comforts and teaches you (John 14:16–17), enables you to obey God (Romans 8:11), and, as Acts 1:8 tells, gives you power to tell others about Him.

Why tell others? Because God doesn't adopt anyone into His family to be an only child.

If you're worried people might mock your faith, it's tempting to distract them from what you really possess—changing a conversation away from God, hiding the fact that you go to church, acting the same as whoever is around you. Yet meeting God as Savior and Lord is like unearthing a limitless, eternal treasure. You've found a Mount Everest of spiritual gold. Don't be too stingy to share it with your friends.

I am proud of the Good News, because it is the power God uses to save everyone who believes—to save the Jews first, and also to save those who are not Jews.

—ROMANS 1:16 NCV

It isn't your job alone to defend your Christian faith. You don't have to rely on your own brainpower and Bible knowledge to answer peers or professors or even parents who argue with you. There's no such thing as a new spiritual question. Check out unbeatable books like these to help answer tough questions and to know more about how to spread God's News:

- **True for You But Not for Me (Paul Copan)**
- **The Compact Guide to World Religions (Dean Halverson)**
- **The Dark Side of the Supernatural (Bill Myers and Dave Wimbish)**

- **What's With the Mutant in the Microscope? (Kevin Johnson and James White)**
- **What's With the Dudes at the Door? (Kevin Johnson and James White)**
- **Don't Check Your Brains at the Door (Josh McDowell and Bob Hostetler).**
- **Evidence That Demands a Verdict (Josh McDowell).**

God's News is something you *live*. It's also something you *say*. But remember: The Good News isn't your message. It's God's message. You don't do the fixing. God does. You speak the News. He does the work.

My job was to plant the seed in your hearts, and Apollos watered it, but it was God, not we, who made it grow. The ones who do the planting or watering aren't important, but God is important because he is the one who makes the seed grow.

—1 CORINTHIANS 3:6–7 NLT

What do ya know? :
248.8 JOHNSON
GLOUCESTER CO LIBRARY SYSTEM